Where Is Maryland?

Where Is Maryland?

by Jennifer Marino Walters

illustrated by Ted Hammond

Penguin Workshop

For Kristi Carbone, one of the greatest travel buddies a girl could ask for!—JMW

PENGUIN WORKSHOP
An imprint of Penguin Random House LLC
1745 Broadway, New York, NY 10019
penguinrandomhouse.com

Designed and Produced by Dinardo Design, LLC.

Library of Congress Cataloging-in-Publication Data is available.

First published in the United States of America by Penguin Workshop, 2026

Manufactured in the United States of America
CJKW

ISBN 9798217244041 (paperback)
10 9 8 7 6 5 4 3 2 1

ISBN 9798217244058 (library binding)
10 9 8 7 6 5 4 3 2 1

The authorized representative in the EU for product safety and compliance is Penguin Random House Ireland, Morrison Chambers, 32 Nassau Street, Dublin D02 YH68, Ireland, https://eu-contact.penguin.ie.

Contents

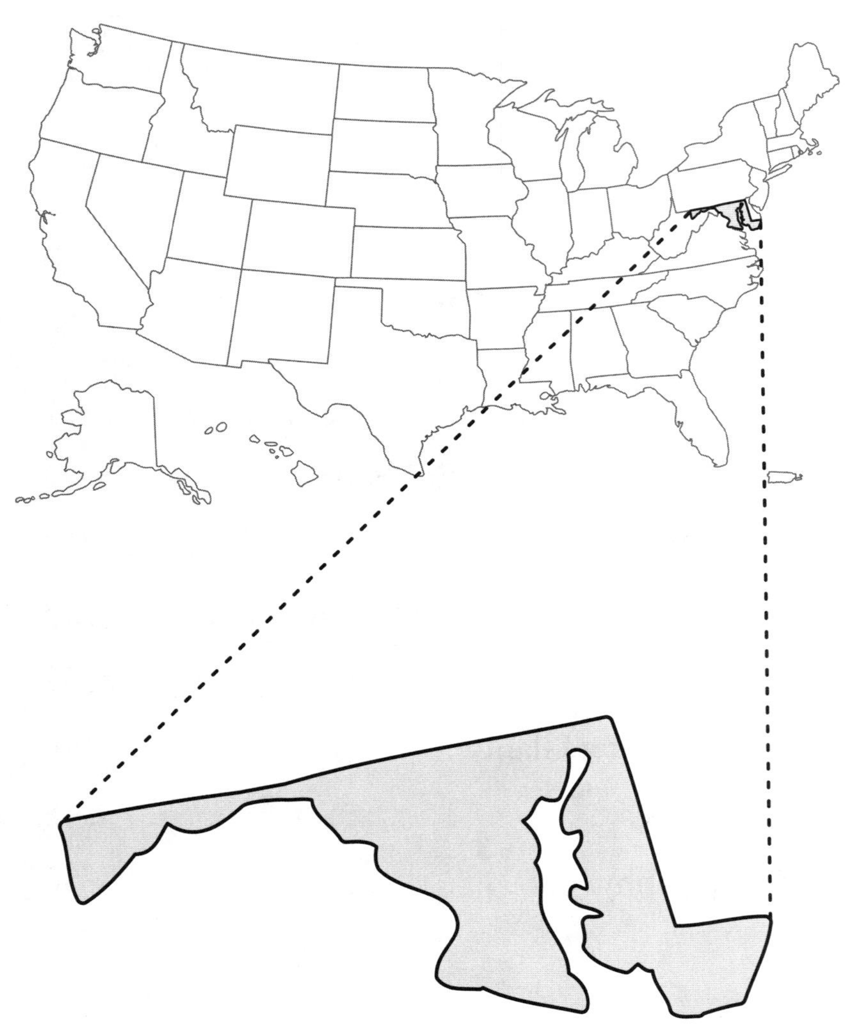

Where Is Maryland?

It was the morning of September 14, 1814. Francis Scott Key, a lawyer from Maryland, was aboard a ship in Baltimore Harbor. The ship was a few miles from Fort McHenry in Baltimore. Throughout the night, English ships fired mortars and rockets at Fort McHenry, where American forces were stationed. They hoped to destroy the fort so they could capture the city of Baltimore. American troops fired back with guns, cannons, rockets, and mortars. "The heavens aglow were a seething sea of flame," Key later wrote when describing the Battle of Baltimore.

Sometime during the night, the battle suddenly ended. All was quiet. But Key could barely see through all the darkness and smoke. He didn't know if his side had won or if the British had destroyed Fort McHenry. In the light of the morning, what he saw filled his heart with joy: The American flag was still flying! The Americans had won the battle. The British troops left the harbor without attacking Baltimore.

Key wrote a poem about the battle. He called it "The Defence of Fort M'Henry." A friend published Key's poem and handed it out to people in Baltimore. Newspapers printed it. People began to sing it to the tune of a song called "To Anacreon in Heaven," and it was renamed "The Star-Spangled Banner." The song soon became a symbol of the United States, the young country's first steps toward independence, and the important role Maryland had to play.

CHAPTER 1
Maryland's Land and Environment

Maryland is located on the East Coast of the United States. It is bordered by Pennsylvania to the north, Delaware and the Atlantic Ocean to the east, the Atlantic Ocean and Virginia to the south, and West Virginia to the west. Maryland's northern border with Pennsylvania is known as the Mason-Dixon Line and considered the boundary between the north and the south of the United States.

Maryland is a small state. Only eight states are smaller! However, it's the nineteenth most populous state. Even with its size, Maryland's landscape is so diverse that it was given the nickname "America in Miniature."

Southern and eastern Maryland—about

half of the state's land area—are on the Atlantic Coastal Plain. The Coastal Plain is divided in the center by the Chesapeake Bay, which makes Maryland's Coastal Plain resemble lobster claws. The bay is the largest estuary (a place where rivers flow into the ocean) in the United States and the third largest in the world. It is home to more than 3,600 species of plants and animals, from marine life such as the blue crab (named for its bright blue claws) to waterbirds such as the blue heron and the osprey.

The portion of Maryland's Coastal Plain east of the Chesapeake Bay is known as the Eastern Shore. Maryland's Eastern Shore is part of the Delmarva Peninsula (a piece of land that's surrounded by water on three sides), named because it contains parts of Delaware, Maryland, and Virginia. The Eastern Shore is flat with many wetlands covered with shallow water. There are also sandy beaches, both on the Atlantic Ocean

side and the Chesapeake Bay side. Ocean City, a popular vacation spot, includes over ten miles of beach and a wooden boardwalk with rides, shops, restaurants, and other attractions.

The Coastal Plain west of the Chesapeake Bay, called the Western Shore, is flat with some low hills. While most of the Coastal Plain is farmland, Maryland's most populous city, Baltimore, is located there. So is Maryland's capital, Annapolis.

West of the Coastal Plain is the Piedmont Plateau (say: PEED-mont plah-TOE), beginning at an area called a fall line, where rivers, rapids, and waterfalls cascade off rocks as they flow toward the ocean. The Piedmont fills much of central Maryland and has many oak forests.

To the west of the Piedmont is a narrow strip of mountains called the Blue Ridge Mountains, which becomes the Appalachian Ridge and Valley. This area has many forests and steep ridges, as well as farmland. The Appalachian Plateau fills the northwestern corner of the state and contains the Allegheny (say: ah-luh-GAY-nee) Mountains. These include Backbone Mountain, which is Maryland's highest point at 3,360 feet.

Western Maryland has a continental climate, meaning it has hot summers and cold winters. The eastern part of the state has a subtropical climate. That means it is hot and humid in the summer and mild (not too cold) in the winter.

The state averages about forty-three inches of precipitation each year.

About 40 percent of Maryland is covered in forests. There are more than 160 tree species in the state, with oak and hickory as the most common. The forested mountains in the west are filled with pine groves (small groups of trees). Swallow Falls State Park in western Maryland is home to the state's oldest grove of eastern hemlock and white pine trees. Many of them are over three hundred years old!

Most of Maryland's rivers flow into the Chesapeake Bay. The three biggest are the Potomac (say: puh-TOE-mik), the Patapsco (say: puh-TAP-sko), and the Patuxent (say: puh-TUCK-sint) Rivers. The Potomac River forms the southern and western border of Maryland, the Patapsco flows through Baltimore, and the Patuxent is the longest river that stays entirely within Maryland.

The Susquehanna (say: sus-kwuh-HAN-uh) River is the longest river on the East Coast of the United States. It flows about five hundred miles from Cooperstown, New York, through Pennsylvania, and into the Chesapeake Bay in northeastern Maryland. The Susquehanna carries in over half of the bay's fresh water.

The Pocomoke River is the easternmost river that flows into the Chesapeake. It drains water

from four counties in Delaware, Virginia, and Maryland.

There are more than one hundred lakes in Maryland, but none of them are natural lakes—they are all human-made, formed by dams built across rivers. The state's largest lake is Deep Creek Lake in the Allegheny Mountains. Deep Creek Lake has an area of 3,900 acres. That's larger than 2,900 football fields!

Maryland is home to about ninety species of mammals, including black bears, bobcats, foxes, coyotes, and white-tailed deer. Assateague (say: ass-uh-TEEG) Island on Maryland's Eastern Shore (a small part of which is in Virginia), as well as the adjacent Chincoteague (say: SHING-kuh-teeg) Island off the coast of Virginia, are home to a famous population of wild ponies. There are over 225 horses on the islands today. Each year in July, people called "saltwater cowboys" round up the horses from the Virginia side of Assateague and help them swim to Chincoteague, where they are examined and given any needed medical care.

Over four hundred bird species live in Maryland, including the Baltimore oriole (Maryland's state bird). The oriole, known for its bright-orange and black feathers, got its name from the Latin word *oriolus*, which means "golden." The state reptile, the diamondback

terrapin, lives along the Eastern Shore and is protected by law. This sea turtle lays its eggs on land, and its babies immediately crawl to the nearest body of water once they hatch.

Marine life abounds in Maryland, even beyond the Chesapeake Bay. Large marine mammals, including bottlenose dolphins, humpback whales, harbor seals, loggerhead turtles, and others, are found in Maryland's ocean waters.

CHAPTER 2
State Origins

The first people to live in the area we call Maryland are believed to have arrived around 10,000 BCE. These people, known as Paleo-Indians, were hunter-gatherers. For food, they hunted large mammals such as mammoths, bison, and caribou, and gathered roots, nuts, berries, and fruit. They moved often to follow the animals they hunted.

The Paleo-Indian culture gave way to Eastern Archaic (say: ar-KAY-ick) people, who grew crops and fished in the Chesapeake Bay. Around 500 BCE, the Adena and Hopewell people settled in Maryland. They were known as Mound Builders because they built huge earth mounds. The Mound Builders disappeared by 1000 CE.

Around the same time, the Archaic culture developed into the Woodland culture, whose people set up small villages along the shores of the bay.

After that, the groups that settled in the area mostly spoke Algonquian (say: al-GON-quee-in) languages. The largest of these Indigenous nations were the Lenni-Lenape (say: LEH-nee LEH-nuh-pee), the Nanticoke (say: nan-TUH-coke), the Piscataway (say: pis-CAT-uh-way), and the Patuxent. They lived in homes made of branches, bark, and mud. The Algonquian groups hunted animals including bears, deer, elk, and turkeys. They also caught fish, crabs, clams, and oysters. They grew squash, corn, and beans to eat, and gathered strawberries, blackberries, nuts, and wild root vegetables.

In 1608, English explorer Captain John Smith sailed into the Chesapeake Bay and spent several weeks mapping the shoreline. In 1631, English fur trader and trapper William Claiborne built a trading post on Kent Island. He gave food and other goods to Indigenous people in exchange for furs from animals, such as beavers, which he could sell in Europe.

An Englishman named George Calvert wanted to start a colony where people could practice their own religions. Calvert was a Roman Catholic and could not worship the way he wanted to in England. After Calvert's death, King Charles I

granted his son Cecil Calvert a charter for the land from the Potomac River up to present-day Philadelphia, even though Indigenous people were already living there. The colony was named Maryland for Charles's wife, Queen Henrietta Maria of France.

After Cecil Calvert died, his brother Leonard Calvert sailed from England to Maryland with two hundred colonists aboard two ships. They arrived at St. Clement's Island in March 1634

and established the town of St. Mary's. As more colonists arrived, the town grew into St. Mary's City, which served as Maryland's capital for more than sixty years. Leonard Calvert was its first governor.

At first, the colonists and Indigenous people had mostly peaceful relationships. Some Indigenous people allowed colonists to use their land, helped them hunt and farm, and traded them furs in exchange for items such as pots, cloth, and tools. The colonists would then sell the furs to people in Europe for large profits.

St. Mary's City began to thrive. Colonists grew crops such as wheat, corn, soybeans, and squash. Tobacco soon became the most important crop. The Chesapeake Bay area became known as the Tobacco Coast by both the colonists and Europeans who wanted to buy tobacco. Tobacco was often used as money in Maryland because it was so valuable.

Wealthy people bought land and set up tobacco plantations (large farms) in the colony. They brought people over from Europe (mainly England and Ireland) to work on the plantations as indentured servants. That meant the plantation owners paid for the workers' journey to Maryland. In return, the workers labored on the plantations

until the cost of their trip was paid off. This often took four or five years!

While most indentured servants were white, some were Black. One of the first indentured servants in Maryland was a man who may have been Cape Verdean, Mathias de Sousa. De Sousa worked for four years as an indentured servant. He later traded with Maryland's Indigenous people. In 1642, de Sousa became the first man of African descent to serve in the Maryland Legislative Assembly.

As the demand for labor grew, the cost of indentured servants went up. Maryland plantation owners realized they could save a lot of money by enslaving people. The first record of enslaved Africans in Maryland was in St. Mary's City in 1642. In 1664, Maryland passed a law that made slavery legal in the colony. Soon, enslaved people completely replaced indentured servants on Maryland's plantations.

Maryland had also passed the Act Concerning Religion, which later came to be known as the Act of Religious Toleration. This law gave all Christians, including both Protestants and Roman Catholics, the right to practice their own religion. This attracted even more people to Maryland.

As more Europeans moved to Maryland and set up plantations, Indigenous people were forced off their lands. They were also being killed by the many diseases the Europeans brought with them, such as measles, smallpox, and plague. They fought with the colonists over land and hunting rights that had been taken from them. By the late 1700s, few Indigenous people remained in Maryland.

England established the colony of Pennsylvania north of Maryland in 1681. Almost immediately, the two colonies began arguing over land. They couldn't agree on where their border would be. The city of Baltimore was founded in 1729 and quickly became an important port, especially for shipping tobacco and grain. Maryland colonists felt they deserved more land. The dispute between Maryland and Pennsylvania was finally settled in 1767 when England (which was now called Great Britain) officially established the border between the two colonies. That boundary was named for its surveyors (people who examine and measure an area of land), Charles Mason and Jeremiah Dixon.

By 1732, there were thirteen British colonies in America. The British tried to take more control of the colonies and introduced new taxes for them to pay. That made the colonists unhappy, and they began to rebel against British rule. This led to the American Revolution, which began in 1775. General George Washington led the Continental Army against the British. Many people from Maryland served in the Continental Army. They were some of the most highly trained troops

and were given very difficult jobs. Washington called them "The Maryland Line." Maryland is sometimes called the "Old Line State" in their honor.

In 1776, the colonies declared independence from Great Britain and formed the United States. But the war didn't officially end until 1783. The US Constitution was written in 1787. Maryland ratified, or approved, it in 1788, officially becoming the seventh US state.

George Washington became the first president of the United States in 1789. He wanted the country to have a capital city that was separate from any state. Maryland and Virginia each gave up part of their land along the Potomac River in 1790 to form the new capital. It was called Washington, District of Columbia, or Washington, DC, for short. It is still the US capital.

CHAPTER 3
Growth and Development

The United States went to war with Great Britain again in 1812. Great Britain was already fighting with France and tried to block US ships from stopping at French ports. The British also sometimes forced sailors from US ships to join the British navy. President James Madison declared war. It was during that war that the famous Battle of Baltimore happened, after which Francis Scott Key wrote "The Star-Spangled Banner." The large flag the song was based on had been stitched by Mary Pickersgill in Baltimore. It now hangs in the Smithsonian's National Museum of American History in Washington, DC.

The war ended in 1815 with no clear winner. But new improvements in transportation and communication helped Maryland grow. The first highway built entirely with US government funds connected the eastern and western states at the time. By 1818, it ran all the way from Cumberland, Maryland, in the east, to Wheeling, Virginia (now part of West Virginia), in the west. Called the National Road, the highway eventually stretched all the way to Vandalia, Illinois, and provided a quicker way for people and products to travel from eastern states to the Midwest.

In 1828, construction began on the first US passenger railroad, the Baltimore and Ohio (B&O) Railroad. The first thirteen miles connected Baltimore and Ellicott's Mills (now Ellicott City) and opened in 1830. The steam-powered train reached speeds of up to fourteen miles per hour and helped people travel more easily than by river or horse! Canals (human-made waterways) also made it easy to move goods between the eastern and western parts of the state.

The Chesapeake and Delaware Canal, which linked the Chesapeake Bay and the Delaware River, opened in 1829.

The first message transmitted on the country's first intercity telegraph line was sent in 1844 from Washington, DC, to Baltimore. (A telegraph is a system using wires and electrical signals to send messages quickly over long distances.) And in 1852, the B&O Railroad became the first rail line to reach from the Eastern Seaboard to the Ohio River.

Maryland's growth, like that of other states, was largely based on the labor of enslaved people of African descent. A secret system called the Underground Railroad grew in the 1800s. The Underground Railroad was not under the ground, and it was not a train. Instead, it was a network of people who helped freedom seekers escape from Southern states and get to Northern states or Canada, where slavery was illegal. Stops along the various routes were called stations, and the people who helped were called conductors.

Tens of thousands of enslaved people escaped

to freedom through the Underground Railroad. It was a difficult and dangerous journey. These people left family members behind and traveled hundreds of miles by foot, in boats, or in wagons with little to no food, clothing, or money. To avoid being caught, they often traveled at night, and sometimes they wore disguises. If they couldn't travel with a conductor, they had to rely on information from other enslaved people about routes and safe places to stop.

Underground Railroad stops could be inside someone's basement or attic, in a barn, or in a crawl space under a church floor. At each stop, freedom seekers would receive food, shelter, and information about where to go next. Many of these Underground Railroad stops were in Maryland. The state's location near the border with the North made it a common stop on the journey to freedom. Enslaved people could also escape via the Chesapeake Bay and its rivers.

Harriet Tubman (Around 1822–1913)

Harriet Tubman was born on a plantation to enslaved parents in Dorchester County around the year 1822. She was named Araminta—"Minty" for short—and was the fifth of nine children. She later changed her name to Harriet in honor of her mother.

Around age twelve, Tubman was hit in the head with an iron weight when she refused to help capture a freedom seeker trying to escape. The weight injured her skull, and the injury caused her health problems for the rest of her life, including painful headaches.

The injury didn't stop Tubman's bravery. In 1849, she escaped to Philadelphia and later returned to her former plantation to rescue family members. Once she did, she wanted to help even more people. She made thirteen trips back to Maryland over the next decade, helping guide about seventy enslaved

people to freedom. She claimed to have never lost a single person she was leading to freedom. Tubman became one of the most famous conductors of the Underground Railroad.

Tubman also served with Union forces in South Carolina during the Civil War. She worked as a scout, a nurse, and a laundress. In 2024, over one hundred years after her death, she was given the rank of Brigadier General in the Maryland National Guard.

There were also many abolitionists (people who work to end slavery) from Maryland. One of the most famous was Frederick Douglass. He was born to an enslaved mother in 1818 on the Eastern Shore, then lived in Baltimore. In 1838, Douglass escaped to the North by dressing as a sailor.

Douglass later traveled the country to speak about abolition. He also wrote three autobiographies and started an abolitionist newspaper called *The North Star*, named after the famous star that freedom seekers used at night to point them north. His home became a station on the Underground Railroad, through which Douglass helped other freedom seekers escape.

The American Civil War began in 1861 over the issue of slavery. Eleven Southern states seceded (removed themselves) from the country to form the Confederacy, with Richmond as its capital. More than twenty other states remained in the

United States and called themselves the Union, led by President Abraham Lincoln. The Union wanted to end slavery. The Confederacy wanted slavery to continue.

Maryland was part of the Union, but not everyone living in the state wanted to be. Most people on the Eastern Shore supported the South, while most in western Maryland supported the Union. Some Maryland Army units fought for the Union while others fought for the Confederacy. Sometimes they even fought against each other.

Several Civil War battles took place in Maryland, including the Battle of Antietam (say: an-TEE-tum), one of the deadliest one-day battles in US military history. On September 17, 1862, Confederate troops led by General Robert E. Lee hoped to capture Washington, DC, but were met at Antietam Creek by the Union army led by General George B. McClellan. Nearly 3,700 soldiers were killed and over 17,000 were wounded before Lee turned his forces back and the Union declared victory. The Civil War ended in 1865, and slavery was abolished (made illegal) by the United States.

Black people had to fight for equal rights in Maryland after slavery was abolished. In 1870, the Fifteenth Amendment to the US Constitution made it illegal for states to deny people the right to vote based on race. People in Maryland still tried to block Black people from voting. (Maryland did not officially ratify the Fifteenth Amendment until 1973.) Maryland also passed Jim Crow laws—laws that enforced racial segregation (the separation of Black people and white people in public spaces) that were common in the South.

Even with these struggles after the Civil War, the state of Maryland prospered, especially Baltimore. The most inland port on the East Coast, it had direct railroad links to the Midwest. New chemical, textile, and canning factories opened. Many immigrants moved to Baltimore from Germany, Ireland, Greece, Italy, Russia, and Poland to work in the city. Baltimore's population nearly doubled from over 260,000 in 1870 to more than 500,000 in 1900.

After the United States entered World War I in 1917, military bases such as Aberdeen Proving Ground and Edgewood Arsenal opened. Fort McHenry greatly expanded. Over sixty-two thousand men and women from Maryland served in the war. During World War II, Baltimore was a major production center for US military aircraft and ships. The US Army tested tanks at Aberdeen Proving Ground, and thousands of men and women served in the military.

Maryland's population grew during and after World War II. Baltimore/Washington International Thurgood Marshall Airport, originally called Friendship International Airport, opened in 1950. Two years later, the eastern and

western portions of the state were connected for the first time by the Chesapeake Bay Bridge. Until then, people had to use ferry boats to travel between the two sides of Maryland. Both the airport and the bridge brought more tourists and businesses to Maryland.

The 1950s saw the rise of the civil rights movement—the fight for equal rights for all people regardless of race, sex, or religion. The movement was led by Black Americans. One of them was Thurgood Marshall, a lawyer from Baltimore. In 1954, he successfully argued *Brown v. Board of Education* before the US Supreme Court, which made segregation in public schools illegal. After that, he argued many more cases in support of civil rights. Ten years later, the Civil Rights Act of 1964 was passed. This federal law prohibited discrimination based on race, color, religion, sex, and national origin, which included segregation. In 1967, Marshall became the first-ever Black US Supreme Court justice.

Pollution was becoming a serious problem in Chesapeake Bay. For many years, factories and towns had emptied waste into rivers that led into the bay. This was affecting Maryland's fishing industry centered on the bay, with blue crab, oysters, and striped bass being some of the largest catches.

In 1980, the Chesapeake Bay Commission was established. This joint commission between Maryland and Virginia, and later Pennsylvania, works to figure out how to reduce pollution in the bay and make it healthier. In 2000, the states signed an agreement to restore and protect Chesapeake Bay resources. They wanted to ensure Maryland's future and the future of the bay's irreplaceable natural resources.

CHAPTER 4
Today's State

Today, most of Maryland's residents live in the areas around Washington, DC, and Baltimore. Many Marylanders work for the federal government. Some of them commute from Southern Maryland into Washington, DC, to work in the government buildings there. Others work at military bases in the state. Joint Base Andrews is the home of Air Force One, the airplane that the president of the United States flies on. Walter Reed National Military Medical Center in Bethesda provides medical care to active duty service members and their families, veterans, and US leaders including the president and vice president.

The Port of Baltimore remains another large

contributor to Maryland's economy. It's one of the twenty largest ports in the United States, where products such as farm and construction equipment, coal, and motor vehicles enter and leave the country.

Agriculture is Maryland's largest commercial industry. Some of the fruits and vegetables grown in Maryland are watermelons, mushrooms, tomatoes, and peas. Dairy and chicken farming

are also big in the state.

Fishing off Maryland's coast is popular for individuals as well as big businesses. More than one-third of the country's blue crabs are caught in the Chesapeake Bay. Maryland crab cakes are a favorite local dish and known around the world! Striped bass and Eastern oysters are also popular with seafood lovers.

More than fifty colleges and universities in

Maryland employ many people. The largest is the University of Maryland, with eleven campuses throughout the state. The main campus of Johns Hopkins University, a top medical school, is in Baltimore. And the United States Naval Academy is in Annapolis. The Colonial Annapolis Historic District has more structures dating from before the American Revolution than any other historic district in the country. The Maryland State House in Annapolis, completed in 1779, is the oldest state capitol in continuous use.

Boating, sailing, and crabbing are common on Chesapeake Bay. People flock to Maryland's beaches in the summer. They can hunt for shark teeth on the beaches of Calvert Cliffs State Park and stroll along the Ocean City Boardwalk. In western Maryland, people can go whitewater rafting, ski, and hike a portion of the famed Appalachian Trail. The mountains of western Maryland are also home to Camp David, the presidential retreat.

Maryland has three major professional sports teams: Major League Baseball's Baltimore Orioles and the National Football League's Baltimore Ravens and Washington Commanders. Car races and horse races take place there. Steeplechasing—a type of horse race that involves jumping over fences and water—became popular in Maryland in the late 1800s and still is. Lacrosse is also big in Maryland—so much so that it was named the state's official team sport in 2004. The USA

Lacrosse headquarters, home to the National Lacrosse Hall of Fame, is in Sparks.

Maryland's official state sport is something much less common—jousting! In the original form of jousting, which became popular around the 1200s, two knights on horseback tried to unseat each other with a lance (a long, pointed weapon). In the modern version of the sport, two opponents on horseback try to spear rings with their lances. Jousting was named the state sport

in 1962 because of its long history in Maryland, dating back to colonial times.

Baltimore's Inner Harbor—full of museums, restaurants, shops, and other attractions—draws many tourists. At the National Aquarium, visitors can see dolphins, sharks, jellyfish, and more. The Maryland Science Center, one of the oldest science museums in the country, has exhibits on dinosaurs, space, the human body, and beyond. Inner Harbor visitors can also explore the three-story Port Discovery Children's Museum, get hands-on at the B&O Railroad Museum, and tour the USS *Constellation*, the last sail-only warship built by the US Navy.

Theater and the arts are also strong in Baltimore. The Baltimore Symphony Orchestra plays at the Joseph Meyerhoff Symphony Hall. The Hippodrome Theatre at the France-Merrick Performing Arts Center hosts Broadway-style shows.

There are over one hundred thousand Indigenous people living in Maryland. Many of them are part of three state-recognized nations—the Piscataway Indian Nation, the Piscataway Conoy Tribe, and the Accohannock Indian Tribe.

From the beaches and waters of the Eastern Shore and the Chesapeake Bay area, to the bustling cities and suburbs of Central Maryland, all the way to the mountains in the west, Maryland's diversity helps it live up to the name "America in Miniature."

Maryland at a Glance

Statehood: 1788

Nickname: Old Line State

Abbreviation: MD

State Motto: *Fatti maschii parole femine*

(Italian for "Manly deeds, womanly words")

State Tree: White oak

State Insect: Baltimore checkerspot butterfly

Capital: Annapolis

Size: 12,406 square miles

Population: Over 6 million

Famous People from Maryland:

Babe Ruth and Cal Ripken Jr. (Hall of Fame baseball players), Jada Pinkett Smith (actress), Michael Phelps (former Olympic swimmer), Toni Braxton (singer)

State flag

State bird

Baltimore oriole

State flower

Black-eyed Susan

FUN FACT:

The crown-shaped bottle cap was invented in Baltimore in 1892 by Maryland native William Painter.

Timeline of Maryland

1631	William Claiborne sets up a trading post on Kent Island
1634	British colonists found the town of St. Mary's
1729	The city of Baltimore is founded
1767	The Mason-Dixon Line is set as Maryland's northern boundary
1788	Maryland becomes the seventh US state
1814	Francis Scott Key writes the poem that becomes "The Star-Spangled Banner"
1828	Construction begins on the B&O Railroad
1862	The Battle of Antietam becomes one of the bloodiest days in US military history
1917	Aberdeen Proving Ground opens
1952	The Chesapeake Bay Bridge opens to traffic
1967	Thurgood Marshall becomes the first Black US Supreme Court justice
1980	The Chesapeake Bay Commission is established to help clean and protect the bay
2004	Lacrosse is named Maryland's official team sport
2024	More than one hundred years after her death, Harriet Tubman is given the rank of Brigadier General in the Maryland National Guard

Timeline of the World

1632	Construction begins on India's Taj Mahal
1714	Daniel Gabriel Fahrenheit invents the first mercury thermometer
1770	Composer Ludwig van Beethoven is born
1789	Citizens storm the Bastille during the French Revolution
1824	Mexico becomes a republic three years after declaring independence from Spain
1845	The Great Famine begins in Ireland, spurring a great migration of people to the United States
1868	The world's first traffic light is used in London
1914	The Panama Canal opens
1954	The Vietnam War begins
1961	Yuri Gagarin of the Soviet Union becomes the first human in space
1977	*Star Wars* opens in movie theaters
2004	A tsunami in the Indian Ocean kills an estimated 228,000 people in fifteen countries
2024	Taylor Swift's Eras Tour earns a record-breaking $2 billion in ticket sales

Bibliography

***Books for young readers**

*Jones Prince, April. ***Who Was Frederick Douglass?*** New York: Penguin Workshop, 2014.

*Mattern, Joanne. ***Fort McHenry: Our Flag Was Still There.*** South Egremont, MA: Red Chair Press, 2017.

*Somervill, Barbara A. ***Maryland.*** New York: Children's Press, 2009.

*Yasuda, Anita. ***What's Great About Maryland?*** Minneapolis: Lerner Publishing Group, 2015.

*Zeldis McDonough, Yona. ***What Was the Underground Railroad?*** New York: Penguin Workshop, 2013.

*Zeldis McDonough, Yona. ***Who Was Harriet Tubman?*** New York: Penguin Workshop, 2019.

Websites

Fort McHenry National Monument and Historic Shrine: www.nps.gov/fomc/index.htm

Harriet Tubman Underground Railroad National Historic Park: www.nps.gov/hatu/index.htm